A HISTORICAL ALBUM OF

CONNECTICUT

A HISTORICAL ALBUM OF

CONNECTICUT

Charles A. Wills

THE MILLBROOK PRESS, Brookfield, Connecticut

*Front and back cover: "Home to Thanksgiving," lithograph by Currier & Ives, 1867.
Library of Congress.*

Title page: Autumn in Connecticut. Courtesy of the Greater Fairfield Tourism District.

Library of Congress Cataloging-in-Publication Data

Wills, Charles.
 A historical album of Connecticut / Charles A. Wills.
  p. cm. — (Historical albums)
 Includes bibliographical references and index.
 Summary: A history of Connecticut, from its early exploration
and settlement to the state today.
 ISBN 1-56294-506-8 (lib. bdg.) ISBN 1-56294-848-2 (pbk.)
 1. Connecticut—History—Juvenile literature. 2. Connecticut—
Gazetteers—Juvenile literature. [1. Connecticut—History] I. Title.
II. Series.
F94.3.W55 1995
974.6—dc20

                                              94-36290
                                                 CIP
                                                  AC

 Created in association with Media Projects Incorporated

   C. Carter Smith, *Executive Editor*
   Lelia Wardwell, *Managing Editor*
   Charles A. Wills, *Principal Writer*
   Bernard Schleifer, *Art Director*
   Shelley Latham, *Production Editor*
   Arlene Goldberg, *Cartographer*

   Special thanks to Douglas Quat, Connecticut Governor's Office, and the
   Honorable John R. H. Blum, Connecticut Commissioner of Agriculture.

CONTENTS

Introduction

In his 1937 survey of American life, *Inside USA*, writer John Gunther called Connecticut "the worthy little state." Connecticut *is* little—at just over 5,000 square miles, it ranks third smallest among the fifty states. Only Rhode Island and Delaware are smaller.

But those 5,000 square miles are packed with history. Connecticut's founding in the 1630s—when Puritan settlers left neighboring Massachusetts to make new lives along the Connecticut River—was the first westward movement in the land that would become the United States. The Connecticut Colony took an early lead in the movement for independence from Britain, and the state played an important part in the Revolutionary War and in the founding of the United States of America.

In the 1800s, Connecticut inventors like Eli Whitney, Samuel Colt, and Seth Thomas put the state in the forefront of the American industrial revolution. By the 20th century, Connecticut was a powerful industrial state whose mills and factories attracted immigrants from all over the world.

Present-day Connecticut is a state of contrasts. Within its borders are affluent suburbs like Greenwich and troubled cities like Bridgeport. In its towns, perfectly preserved colonial houses often stand across the street from high-tech office parks. With 3 million residents, Connecticut is among the most crowded states—and yet airline pilots say that northeast Connecticut, the state's "quiet corner," is one of the last places on the East Coast where few lights are visible from the air at night.

Not many states can match the diversity of Connecticut in people and landscape, and hardly any other states have had more of an impact on the rest of the nation. For such a small state, then, Connecticut has a remarkably big history.

PART ONE

THE CONSTITUTION STATE

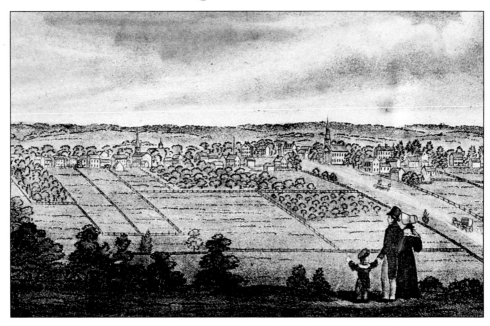

This view of Litchfield in the early 1800s shows the impact of settlement on Connecticut's landscape: Forests have been cleared for farmland, roads extend through the valley, and church spires rise amid the hills.

Dutch fur traders were the first Europeans to explore present-day Connecticut. In the early 1630s, English Puritans from the Massachusetts Bay Colony began to move westward, settling along the Connecticut River and on the shores of Long Island Sound. By the 18th century, the Connecticut Colony was thriving. Following the Revolutionary War, Connecticut's population fell as people left the crowded state. At the same time, however, a group of remarkable inventors—including Eli Whitney, Samuel Colt, Seth Thomas, and Charles Goodyear—helped transform Connecticut from a rural state into the nation's leading producer of manufactured goods.

Connecticut's Native Americans

Connecticut's 5,000 square miles were formed over millions of years by the action of wind, water, and especially glaciers—slow-moving rivers of ice. When the glaciers moved north about 10,000 years ago, they left behind a lovely land of wooded hills dotted with lakes, marshes, and rivers.

Through the middle of Connecticut flows a major river that empties into Long Island Sound. The Native Americans who lived in the region called their homeland *Quinnehtukqt*, or "the land on the long river"—the source of the state's name.

When the first European explorers arrived in the 1600s, Connecticut was home to between 7,000 and 10,000 Native Americans. Like many Indian groups who lived in the forests of northeastern North America, they spoke the Algonquian language.

Four major Native American nations lived in Connecticut. The Sequins lived along the banks of the Connecticut River. The northeastern part of the state was home to the Nipmuc nation. In western Connecticut, along the present-day New York-Connecticut border, lived the Matabesecs. Central and southeastern Connecticut was the territory of the Pequots. All of these nations were made up of many small tribes, each led by one or more *sachems* (leaders).

Native American life centered on the village—a cluster of long bark houses, often protected by a fence of sharpened stakes. These villages were usually built along rivers, or on the shores of Long Island Sound, because these waters provided an abundance of fish and shellfish.

Connecticut's forests were full of deer, turkey, and other game. From the soil came crops of corn, pumpkins, beans, and squash. Hunting was done by the men in each village. Tending crops was usually women's work.

Connecticut's Native Americans lived in a rich land, but often their lives were far from peaceful. To the west, in what is now New York, lived the Mohawks, one of the five nations of the powerful Iroquois Confederacy. Mohawk war parties frequently raided deep into Connecticut. In Connecticut itself, the powerful Pequots often attacked the tribes of the Connecticut River Valley.

In the early 1600s, warfare between different Indian nations made it difficult for Connecticut's people to unite in the face of an even greater danger—the coming of the Europeans.

Between 3,000 and 10,000 years ago, the Native Americans of southeastern New England, including Connecticut, discovered how to make pottery from clay. These clay pots are from the region and were made about AD 1400.

Samuel de Champlain of France explored the New England coast between 1604 and 1607. This engraving (right) of two Native American warriors, taken from a 1613 account of Champlain's voyages, is one of the first European views of the region's people.

Puritans and Pequots

The first European to explore Connecticut was Adriaen Block, a Dutch sea captain. In 1613, Block arrived at the tiny Dutch settlement of New Amsterdam—now New York City. The following year Block and his men built a small ship, the *Onrust* (*Restless*), and sailed it across Long Island Sound.

Block took the *Onrust* up the Connecticut River as far as the modern town of Enfield, where he loaded the ship with furs before returning to New Amsterdam. His cargo thrilled Dutch authorities; furs brought high prices in the markets of Europe.

Dutch fur traders soon arrived in Connecticut, trading tools and other goods to the Native Americans in return for the skins of beavers and other animals. In 1633, a trader named Jacob Van Curler built a small trading post, the House of Hope, not far from present-day Hartford. (The Dutch would abandon the fort in 1654.) But it was England, not Holland, that took the lead in colonizing Connecticut.

England became a Protestant nation in 1534, when the Church of England was formed. However, many people disagreed with church teachings because they felt the Church of England stressed too many Roman Catholic beliefs and rituals. In the early 1600s, some English Protestants left the Church of England. Seeking the freedom to worship in their own way, a few of these "separatists"—or Pilgrims, as they came to be called—crossed the Atlantic in 1620 to found Plymouth Colony in Massachusetts.

Others remained in England, hoping to "purify" the English church from within; thus, these people were called Puritans. In 1630, however, thousands of Puritans began leaving England to settle in Massachusetts.

In 1631, Waginacut, sachem of a Sequin tribe, visited the newly founded Massachusetts Bay Colony. Waginacut's people were at war with the Pequots, and the sachem wanted the Englishmen's help in the conflict. He invited the Puritan leaders to

send settlers to the Connecticut River Valley.

Two years passed, however, before Massachusetts Puritans began to move into Connecticut. In 1633, an expedition led by William Holmes set up a trading post a few miles from the House of Hope. Soon afterward, several families from Massachusetts arrived nearby to found Windsor, Connecticut's first English town. The following year, another Massachusetts man, John Oldham, established the town of Wethersfield.

The prospect of moving to Connecticut appealed to Thomas Hooker, a Puritan minister with a church in New Town (now Cambridge), Massachusetts. After arriving in Massachusetts in 1633, Hooker found himself

This 19th-century woodcut (opposite) depicts a Puritan couple. Puritan dress was generally plain and modest, especially on Sundays. Although they were simple, daily clothes weren't usually drab. Puritans favored bright colors like red, yellow, blue, and green.

Driving their livestock onward, Thomas Hooker and his followers walk toward their new home on the Connecticut River in the spring of 1636 in this engraving (above). A small "advance party" of settlers had already arrived at the future site of Hartford late in 1635.

at odds with the colony's leaders over his religious and political beliefs.

Thus, in the spring of 1636, Hooker and about 100 people left Massachusetts to set up their own settlement. Walking overland, Hooker and his followers arrived on the banks of the Connecticut River and founded Hartford.

War swept the Connecticut River Valley just months later. It began, as did so many conflicts between white settlers and Indians, with a misunderstanding. In 1634, and again in 1636, Native Americans killed a group of English traders in the valley. The settlers thought the Pequots were responsible. They probably weren't, but the English attacked Pequot villages in revenge. The Pequots, in turn, began raiding English settlements.

The settlers assembled a force of about 100 men under the leadership of Captain John Mason. They were joined by Uncas, the sachem of the Mohegan tribe of the Pequots, and several hundred Narragansett Indians from Rhode Island, who were traditional enemies of the Pequots.

On the morning of May 26, 1637, the Englishmen and their allies surrounded a Pequot village near present-day Mystic. The attackers set the village on fire; between 600 and 700 Pequots died horribly in the blaze. The destruction of the village finally broke the Pequots' power forever.

This engraving shows the English settlers and their Native American allies attacking the main Pequot village in May 1637. In his account of the massacre that followed, Captain John Mason wrote, "Thus the Lord was pleased to smite [destroy] our enemies, and give us their land for an inheritance."

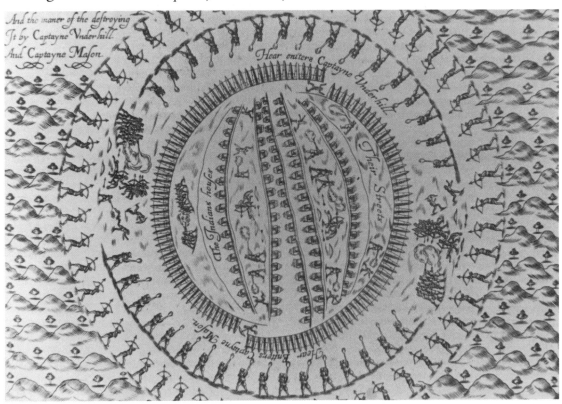

A Spirit of Independence

In the mid-1630s, two more English settlements joined the "three river towns" of Windsor, Wethersfield, and Hartford.

In 1635, English businessmen set up Saybrook Plantation at the mouth of the Connecticut River. Saybrook's founders planned the colony as a haven for wealthy Puritans facing persecution in England, but not many Puritans settled in the colony. Instead, it served as a trading post, and a fort was built to warn the Dutch to keep out of the area.

Three years later, another group of Massachusetts Puritans arrived in Connecticut. Their leaders were Theo-philus Eaton, a merchant, and John Davenport, a clergyman. Like Thomas Hooker, Eaton and Davenport disagreed with the Bay Colony's leaders—but while Hooker felt Massachusetts's religious authorities were too strict, Eaton and Davenport believed the Boston brand of Puritanism was not strict enough.

In the spring of 1638, Eaton and Davenport brought two shiploads of

Many towns sprang up along the Connecticut River (in both the Massachusetts and Connecticut colonies). The maker of this 17th-century map (below) oriented the map with the North directional at the right of the image—not at the top, where it is usually found.

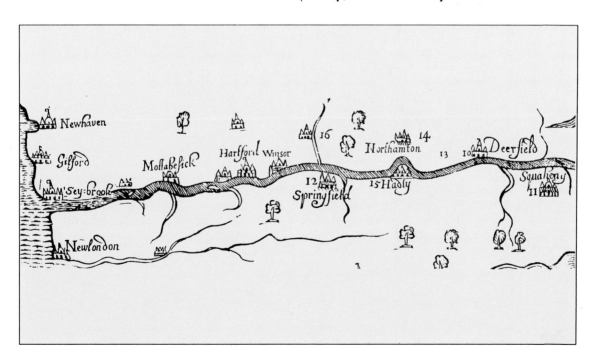

settlers to the shores of Long Island Sound at the mouth of the Quinnipiac River. In 1640, the Quinnipiac Colony changed its name to New Haven.

The three river towns of Windsor, Wethersfield, and Hartford joined together in 1636 as the Connecticut Colony. In 1639, the colony adopted a farsighted set of laws, the Fundamental Orders of Connecticut, as the basis of its government.

The Fundamental Orders had their roots in a sermon preached by Thomas Hooker in 1638. "The foundation of authority," said Hooker, "is laid, firstly, in the free consent of the people." This democratic idea—that the people should have a say in how they are governed—was radical for the time. Drafted by Hooker and Roger Ludlow, a lawyer, the Fundamental Orders were adopted in a meeting at Hartford on January 14, 1639.

By modern standards, the Fundamental Orders weren't very democratic—only men with property were allowed to vote, for example. Still, the Fundamental Orders were a major step forward for democracy in the future United States. Hooker's words would be echoed in the Declaration of Independence.

Connecticut was still ultimately ruled by England, however, and the colony could have only as much self-government as the English crown would allow. In 1660, a new king, Charles II, took power. Charles was unfriendly toward the Puritans, and Connecticut's leading citizens feared he would declare the Fundamental Orders illegal.

In 1661, Connecticut governor John Winthrop, Jr., traveled to England to meet with the king. Happily, Charles II not only confirmed the Fundamental Orders, but granted the colony a royal charter giving the colony the freedom to run its own affairs. The charter also expanded Connecticut's borders to include the New Haven Colony.

A quarter-century later, a threat to Connecticut's freedom arose in the form of Sir Edmund Andros, the royal governor of New York. Andros wanted to unite all of New England under his rule. To do this, he needed to seize Connecticut's charter. Accompanied by soldiers, Andros arrived in Hartford in the fall of 1687 for a tense meeting with the colony's leaders, who bitterly opposed the governor's plans.

What happened next is unknown, but according to a later account, "The charter was brought and laid upon the table. . . . The lights were instantly extinguished, and one Captain Wadsworth, of Hartford, in the most silent and secret manner, carried off the charter, and secreted [hid] it in a large hollow [oak] tree."

However it happened, the charter stayed out of Andros's hands until the governor's plans collapsed, and the story of the "Charter Oak" became part of Connecticut folklore.

The son of the first governor of the Massachusetts Bay Colony, John Winthrop, Jr. (opposite), was governor of the Connecticut Colony for almost twenty years. A talented scientist as well as an able political leader, Winthrop dabbled in astronomy, medicine, and mining.

This 19th-century engraving (below) shows the "Charter Oak," the legendary hiding place of Connecticut's charter during the struggle against Edmund Andros. A fierce storm finally toppled the Hartford tree in August 1856.

The Growth of Colonial Connecticut

Connecticut grew rapidly in the 17th century. In 1640, fewer than 1,000 people lived in the region, including those who settled at Saybrook and New Haven. By 1700, about 30,000 people called Connecticut home.

Most of the colony's people lived in the Connecticut River Valley, where the best farmland was found, or on the coast, where settlers could make a living through fishing and trade. During this time, Connecticut had two capitals: The colony's legislature took turns meeting at New Haven and at Hartford.

In the 1600s, Connecticut's boundaries were unclear. The royal charter of 1662 not only gave the colony large slices of modern-day Rhode Island and New York, but set its western border at the Pacific Ocean! Thus, border disputes with neighboring colonies were an ongoing problem.

New York, for example, claimed the town of Greenwich, while Massachusetts was sure that Stonington, on Long Island Sound at the opposite end of the colony, was in its territory. Both these claims were finally decided in Connecticut's favor, but the colony never succeeded in gaining control of the vast territory granted by the charter of 1662.

As in the rest of New England, the Puritan church was central to colonial life. And while Connecticut was more tolerant than Massachusetts in matters of religion, the colony could be an uncomfortable place for people who didn't share Puritan beliefs. Quakers, for example, were driven from the colony in the 1600s. Connecticut was also the first colony to put people on trial for practicing witchcraft. In 1647, a convicted witch was hung in Connecticut—forty-five years before the more famous witch trials in Salem, Massachusetts.

Along with Connecticut's commitment to the Puritan religion came a commitment to education. The Puritans believed that all people should be able to read the Bible, and they wanted well-educated ministers for their churches. The first grammar school in Connecticut opened in 1637; thirteen years later, the colony's legislature passed a law requiring each town to provide for and build a public school for children.

The colony lacked a college until 1702, when the Reverend Abraham Pierson opened a "collegiate school" at Killingworth (the present-day town of Clinton). In 1716, the college moved to New Haven. Two years later it took the name Yale College after Elihu Yale, a wealthy merchant, donated money for its support. From this small beginning grew

This illustration (above) shows Yale College, as it appeared toward the end of the 18th century. Among Yale's early graduates were the religious leaders Jonathan Edwards (class of 1720) and Samuel Seabury (class of 1748), Noah Webster (class of 1778), editor of *The American Dictionary of the English Language*, and the great inventor Eli Whitney (class of 1792).

With a mule carrying his merchandise—tin dishes and pots, pins, needles, and perhaps a clock or two—a Yankee peddler calls out for customers in this woodcut (right). More often than not, however, peddlers carried their wares on their back. Some colonial peddlers traveled routes as long as 1,500 miles.

This painting shows a ferry with a wagonload of hay crossing a marsh near Old Lyme. Connecticut farmers grew corn, wheat, and vegetables for food, flax to make linen, and sometimes tobacco as a cash crop.

one of the greatest universities in the United States.

By the first decades of the 18th century, Connecticut had grown from a handful of towns to a prosperous colony. Ships sailing from Connecticut ports did a brisk business trading around the world. The spice trade with the West Indies was a major source of wealth for the colony—so much so that Connecticut gained the nickname the Nutmeg State.

Spices and other products were sold door-to-door throughout the colonies by peddlers from Connecticut. The "Yankee peddler" with his sack was a familiar site in colonial America.

The sea was another mainstay of the colony's economy. Every coastal town had its fishing fleet. Whalers from Stonington, New London, and other ports sailed out into the Atlantic to hunt sperm whales for their oil, which was used as fuel for lamps.

Most of the colony's people, however, made their living from the soil, not the sea. Apart from the Connecticut River Valley, Connecticut's soil tended to be thin and rocky, so farming in colonial Connecticut meant dawn-to-dusk work for all family members.

Revolutionary Connecticut

During the 1700s, Britain fought several wars with its European rivals, chiefly France, for control of North America. Britain was victorious, but the financial cost of victory was high. To pay off its wartime debts and raise money to defend its empire, the British Parliament began taxing its North American colonies.

The first major tax, the Stamp Act, became law in 1765. It required colonists to buy special seals to stamp on newspapers and legal documents. Word of the act sparked fiery protests in the colonies. What right did the British government have to impose such a tax, many leading colonists argued, when the colonies weren't represented in Parliament?

Protest was especially strong in Connecticut, where a patriotic society, the Sons of Liberty, organized to fight the tax. Similar groups soon sprang up in other colonies. In September 1765, nearly 500 Sons of Liberty halted Jared Ingersoll, Connecticut's

The Stamp Act's authors carry the law to its grave in this 1767 British cartoon. Because the controversy over the Stamp Act disrupted trade with the colonies, many people in Britain were glad to see the act repealed.

tax agent, on the road to Hartford. The mob forced Ingersoll to resign his post and denounce the act.

This protest and others throughout the colonies forced Parliament to reconsider the Stamp Act, and in 1766 the law was repealed. Over the next decade, however, new taxes increased the tension between Britain and its colonies. By 1774, when Parliament closed the port of Boston as punishment for the famous Boston Tea Party, Connecticut's legislature had begun stockpiling weapons and training Connecticut men for war.

In Connecticut, Patriot sentiment was strongest among the farmers who lived east of the Connecticut River. In the more prosperous western half of the colony, many urged moderation in the growing struggle against Britain. But Connecticut's governor, Jonathan Trumbull, was an outspoken Patriot, and other prominent citizens like Eliphalet Dyer and Israel Putnam took a strong anti-British stance.

On April 19, 1775, British troops clashed with Patriots at Lexington and Concord, Massachusetts, beginning the Revolutionary War. Israel Putnam, a tough old veteran of the wars against the French and Native Americans, was plowing a field when news of the battles at Lexington and Concord reached his farm. He left his plow standing in the field and hurried to Massachusetts to join the fight, bringing nearly 4,000 Connecticut volunteers with him.

Another Connecticut resident, Benedict Arnold of New Haven, also distinguished himself in the early days of the war. Together with Ethan Allen of Vermont, Arnold led a small force that captured Fort Ticonderoga, an important British outpost in New York. Cannons captured from Ticonderoga eventually helped the colonists force the British to sail away from Boston.

When the fighting shifted from Massachusetts to New York, a young Yale graduate named Nathan Hale gave the Patriot cause an enduring example of bravery and sacrifice. Captured while spying behind British lines in September 1776, Hale was sentenced to hang. As he was led to his death, Hale is reputed to have said, "I only regret that I have but one life to give for my country."

By then, the fight against Britain had become a war for American independence. In July 1776, delegates to the Continental Congress formally declared "the United States of America" independent from Great Britain. Among the signers of the declaration were four delegates from Connecticut—Samuel Huntington, Roger Sherman, William Williams, and Oliver Wolcott.

Connecticut, a stronghold of pro-independence feeling, received news of the declaration with joyful celebration. (Connecticut had its share of Tories—pro-British colonists—but there were fewer of them in the

General Israel Putnam escapes from an on-coming Redcoat patrol in this 19th-century lithograph (right). "Old Put," as he was called, was nearly sixty when he left his farm to join the Patriot forces in 1775; bad health forced his retirement from the Continental Army in 1779.

A 19th-century engraving (below) depicts twenty-one-year-old Nathan Hale uttering his famous last words to the British officer in charge of his execution. Hale was a schoolteacher in New London before joining the Continental Army and volunteering for the spying mission that cost him his life.

Simsbury's dismal Newgate Prison was used to house criminals from the end of the Revolutionary War until 1827. A convicted counterfeiter drew this view of the prison around 1800.

Connecticut region than in most other states.)

Seven long years of war lay ahead, however, before American independence became a reality. No major battles were fought on Connecticut soil, but the state endured several destructive British raids.

In April 1777, a British force attacked Danbury, burning the town and capturing or destroying supplies bound for the Continental Army, the chief Patriot fighting force. Two years later, the British returned to Connecticut, this time attacking Norwalk and New Haven.

In troops and supplies, Connecticut's contribution to the Patriot cause was out of proportion to its size. Between 25,000 and 30,000 Connecticut men served in the Continental Army—more than any other state except Massachusetts.

George Washington, the army's commander, could always depend on "Brother Jonathan" Trumbull in Connecticut for much-needed shipments of beef, grain, gunpowder, and other supplies for his often underfed, under-equipped soldiers. Connecticut's farms and workshops provided so much in terms of goods and supplies for the war effort that the state won a new nickname—the Provision

State. Connecticut also provided a major prison for Tories and captured British soldiers. These unfortunate men were jailed in an old copper mine near the town of Simsbury. The underground jail, described by a visitor as a place of "foul vermin, reeking filth and horrible stench," was among the worst prisons kept by either side during the Revolutionary War.

Seagoing Connecticut did its part, too. Coastal towns outfitted scores of privateers—armed merchant ships authorized to attack British shipping. During the war, Connecticut's privateers captured more than 500 British vessels, putting a big dent in the British army's supply line.

In September 1781, Connecticut suffered its last and bloodiest British raid—a two-pronged assault on New London and Groton. The British forces easily captured Fort Trumbull, which guarded New London, and then burned the town. When the British assaulted Fort Griswold outside Groton, however, the Patriot garrison held them off for hours, although the British outnumbered the defenders by at least six to one. When the fort finally fell, the British killed about seventy-five Patriot prisoners in cold blood.

To Connecticut's Patriots, the New London-Groton raid was especially hateful because the British commander was none other than Benedict Arnold. Once a leading Patriot general, Arnold had pledged loyalty to the British in 1779.

While Connecticut recovered from the raid, a combined Patriot-French force (France had joined the war on the Patriot side in 1777) trapped a British army at Yorktown, Virginia. The British surrender at Yorktown in October marked the end of major fighting, and two years later a peace treaty officially recognized the independence of the United States.

While a major general in the Continental Army assigned to command at West Point, Benedict Arnold offered to betray the fort to the British for £20,000. The plot was discovered in time, but Arnold escaped to a British warship. For the remainder of the war he served as a brigadier general for the British, conducting raids in Virginia and Connecticut.

Connecticut and the New Nation

Soon after the surrender at Yorktown, Connecticut joined the other New England states in ending slavery within its borders. In 1784, the state government adopted a policy of gradual emancipation (freedom): Every child born into slavery would be freed at the age of twenty-five.

Other important issues faced the new nation in the years following the Revolutionary War. The United States was independent, but the states were hardly united. Under the Articles of Confederation, adopted by the Continental Congress in 1777, each state was practically its own nation. There was no central government, no national army, and no national financial system.

Many Americans wanted things this way. They believed a strong central government with power over the individual states would lead to the same kinds of abuses the thirteen colonies had originally rebelled against. There were others, however, who felt

some form of central government was needed, or the new nation would fall apart. "I now see anarchy and confusion every day gaining ground among us," wrote Israel Putnam to a friend.

In the summer of 1787, delegates from twelve of the thirteen states met in Philadelphia to hammer out the framework of a new national government. Connecticut sent three delegates —Oliver Ellsworth, William Samuel Johnson, and Roger Sherman—to this constitutional convention.

One of the greatest debates of the convention centered on representation in the two houses of the proposed national legislature, or Congress—the House of Representatives and the Senate. Some delegates from the larger states argued that representation should be based on a state's population. Naturally, delegates from the smaller states opposed this proposal, because it would allow the more populous states to dominate Congress.

Roger Sherman found a solution to this tough problem. He outlined what came to be known as the "Connecticut compromise." Under its terms, each state would have two senators, regardless of its size, while the number of representatives would be determined by its population. The importance of the compromise is one of the reasons (along with the Fundamental Orders) that Connecticut is called the Constitution State.

The Constitution drafted at the convention still had to be ratified

(approved) by the states, however, before it became the law of the land. In January 1788, delegates from Connecticut's towns met at Hartford to debate ratification. On January 9, the delegates ratified the Constitution by a margin of three to one. By the end of the year the document achieved ratification by the required number

Connecticut's debate over ratification of the U.S. Constitution is the theme of this 1787 cartoon (opposite). The state is shown as a wagon being pulled in opposite directions by Federalists (supporters of the Constitution) and antifederalist opponents.

Born in Massachusetts in 1721, Roger Sherman (below) walked 150 miles to Milford, Connecticut, where he settled in 1743. Sherman was the only person to sign all four major documents of the founding of the United States: The Articles of Association, the Declaration of Independence, the Articles of Confederation, and the U.S. Constitution.

of states, and in 1789 George Washington took office as the first president of the United States.

The Constitution put the new nation on a firm footing. Still, the last decade of the 18th century and the first two decades of the 19th century saw Connecticut caught up in several political and military struggles.

In the early 1800s, Britain and France were at war. In 1807, seeking to keep the United States out of the conflict, President Thomas Jefferson forbade American ships to sail for foreign ports. To New England states like Connecticut, which depended heavily on shipping and overseas trade, Jefferson's embargo was an economic disaster.

Opposition to the embargo was political as well as economic: Connecticut and its neighbors were a stronghold of the Federalist Party, which opposed the policies of Jefferson's Republican Party.

Tensions between Britain and the United States continued to rise anyway, and in 1812 Jefferson's successor, James Madison, managed to convince Congress to declare war on Britain. The War of 1812 was unpopular in Connecticut and the rest of New England—so unpopular that Connecticut's government refused to send militia (state troops) to fight in "Mr. Madison's War."

When a British fleet appeared off the coastal town of Stonington in August 1814, however, Connecticut's citizens proved ready to defend themselves. Hastily assembled militia and townspeople kept British troops from landing, and artillery fire from shore killed nearly 100 British sailors and crippled the warship *Despatch*.

From December 1814 to December 1815, Federalist politicians from Connecticut, Massachusetts, Rhode Island, Vermont, and New Hampshire met in Hartford to discuss their dissatisfaction with the war and the Madison administration. The convention proposed amending the Constitution in ways that would take federal power away from Madison and the Republicans.

Critics of the convention accused the Federalist delegates of proposing that New England secede (withdraw) from the United States. These charges, however, were greatly exaggerated.

The Hartford Convention turned out to be an embarrassment for New England and the Federalists: A peace treaty with Britain was signed while the convention was still in session.

In 1818, Hartford was again the site of a major political meeting. This time the issue wasn't war, but a new state constitution for Connecticut. The new constitution extended the right to vote to most of the state's male citizens, and it firmly separated church and state by ending government financial support for the Congregational church. With this action, the last traces of the old Puritan colony passed into history.

Inventors, Industry, and Immigration

Connecticut also experienced great social change as the 18th century gave way to the 19th century.

From the mid-1700s on, Connecticut underwent a population explosion, mostly due to high birthrates in colonial families. About 110,000 people lived in Connecticut in 1750; by 1790, when the first national census was taken, the state's population was nearly 237,000.

This may not sound like much, but in those days most people lived on farms and depended on the land for their livelihood. Unfortunately, there just wasn't enough good farmland in Connecticut to support a large and growing population. As a result, thousands of people left Connecticut to settle in other regions. This exodus began in the 1770s and 1780s, when many Connecticut families migrated to the Berkshire Mountains of western Massachusetts, to upstate New York, and into the disputed territory that became the state of Vermont.

Following the Revolutionary War the tide of migration rose, and in the early 1800s that tide turned into a flood. Some historians estimate that three quarters of a million people left

This engraving of the "Green Woods" around Salisbury and Canaan shows the rocky and hilly terrain of the state's northwest corner in the early 19th century. Lack of good farmland led hundreds of thousands of people to leave Connecticut.

Connecticut between 1783 and 1819. For many Connecticut people, the destination was the Western Reserve, a tract of land along Lake Erie—all that remained of the vast western territory granted to Connecticut in its colonial charter. Many of the pioneers who settled the Western Reserve were veterans of the Continental Army, or families who had lost their homes in British raids during the war.

But for those who stayed behind, Connecticut would soon offer plenty of opportunity for prosperity.

As early as the colonial era, "Connecticut Yankees" were famous for their mechanical skills. In the 19th century, Connecticut's inventors and businesspeople played leading roles in

Eli Whitney (above, left) became an inventor at an early age. As a teenager, he set up a workshop in his family's barn and produced nails and other metal goods, which he sold to neighbors. Young Whitney soon saved enough money to put himself through Yale.

This engraving (left) shows slaves using Whitney's cotton gin. The cotton gin revolutionized cotton cultivation in the South and led to a textile boom in England, but Whitney didn't make much money from his invention. He applied for a patent in 1794, but it wasn't granted until 1807; in the meantime scores of competitors copied his design.

By the 1860s, Samuel Colt's Patent Fire-Arms Manufacturing Company occupied the sprawling Hartford plant shown in this lithograph (opposite). Eli Whitney's son, Eli Whitney, Jr., helped Colt perfect the production methods used to turn out his repeating weapons.

the Industrial Revolution that transformed American society.

The first great invention to come out of Connecticut, however, did more to help the slave-based agriculture of the South than the factories and workshops of New England.

In 1792, a newly graduated Yale man, Eli Whitney, visited a cotton plantation in Georgia. His host, Mrs. Nathanael Greene, urged Whitney to design a machine that would separate cotton fiber from its seed—a long, hard process when done by hand.

Whitney rose to the challenge and designed a cotton gin ("gin" was short for "engine"), which separated fiber from seed quickly and easily. By making cotton a more profitable crop, however, Whitney's cotton gin helped lay the foundation for the "Cotton Kingdom" that developed in the slave-owning Southern states.

Whitney was just one of a host of great Connecticut inventors. Starting in 1802, Eli Terry, Seth Thomas, and Chauncey Jerome applied Whitney's methods to clockmaking. In 1836, Samuel Colt invented the Colt revolver, the first practical repeating firearm. The factory Colt soon built to manufacture his "six-shooters" established Hartford's important arms industry.

Daniel Holmes of Waterbury invented an improved process for making pins and pipes from brass in 1828. Within a few years, Waterbury was famous across the nation as the "Brass City." In 1839, Charles Goodyear of New Haven developed the vulcanization process, a procedure that revolutionized the rubber-manufacturing industry.

The first steam-powered factory in the United States opened in Middletown in 1812. By the middle of the century, mills, factories, and workshops dotted Connecticut's landscape.

Many of the men and women—and children, for there were no child-labor laws at this time—who provided the labor for this American industrial revolution were not native-born Yankees, but newly arrived immigrants.

New England experienced its first great wave of immigration in the 1840s, when hundreds of thousands of Irish people fled poverty and starvation in their homeland. Many found work—hard, often dangerous work that lasted twelve or more hours a day, six or seven days a week—in the factories of Hartford and Waterbury and the textile mills of the Naugatuck Valley.

While industry thrived in inland Connecticut, the state's coastal towns prospered from trade, from whaling, and from seal hunting. The years before the Civil War were the golden age of American whaling, and ports like Mystic and New London sent scores of whaling ships on long voyages in search of oil-rich sperm whales. Stonington's specialty was sealing—hunting seals, valued for their warm skins—in polar waters. It was on an 1819 seal hunting voyage from Stonington that twenty-year-old Captain Nathaniel Palmer became the first person to see the continent of Antarctica.

The 19th century also saw the rise of the insurance industry in Connecticut. Hartford businesspeople began selling insurance to ship captains as early as the 1790s, and in 1810 the first fire insurance company was organized in the city.

It took a disaster in another state to make insurance a mainstay of Connecticut's economy. In 1835, a fire devastated New York City. New York's insurance companies couldn't cope with the flood of claims, but Eliphalet Terry's Hartford Fire Insurance Company swiftly paid its policy holders, allowing hundreds of New York businesses to rebuild. Hartford has been America's insurance capital ever since.

GROWTH AND CHANGE

In this 1876 painting, horse-drawn streetcars and carriages pass by Bridgeport's Burroughs building, which housed offices and shops. At the time, this bustling city's mayor was the legendary showman and circus promoter P. T. Barnum.

Connecticut was an industrial powerhouse in the post-Civil War era. The state's booming economy drew hundreds of thousands of immigrants from all over the world. Connecticut suffered greatly in the Depression years of the 1930s, but World War II saw Connecticut's defense-related industries thrive, and later prosperous suburbs sprang up throughout the state. In the late 1980s and early 1990s, Connecticut endured hard times as manufacturing declined and crime, unemployment, and poverty rose in its cities. Today, the state is exploring innovative solutions to its economic and social problems.

Abolitionism and the Civil War

Connecticut in the middle of the 19th century was a small state with a big influence on the nation.

French philosopher Alexis de Tocqueville, who traveled all over the United States in the 1800s, neatly summed up Connecticut's position. The state, said de Tocqueville, was home to ". . . the clock peddler, the schoolmaster, and the senator. The first gives you the time, the second tells you what to do with it, and the third makes your law and civilization."

The greatest issue facing American civilization in the mid-1800s was slavery. Many Connecticut men and women played important roles in the struggle against slavery and in the terrible Civil War that finally freed the nation's slaves.

As in the rest of New England, Connecticut's people generally opposed slavery—or at least felt that slavery shouldn't be allowed to spread to the new Western states and territories. This antislavery feeling, however, did not mean that free blacks in Connecticut, who numbered between 8,000 and 10,000 in the years before the Civil War, enjoyed equality with white citizens.

In 1833, for example, a young Quaker schoolteacher named Prudence Crandall began teaching black girls in the town of Canterbury. After a few months, an angry mob forced Crandall's school to shut down.

A small but active group of men and women in Connecticut and elsewhere worked tirelessly to end slavery. Because they wanted to abolish (totally eliminate) slavery in the United States, these people were known as abolitionists.

Connecticut's abolitionists scored a small victory in the fight against slavery in the *Amistad* case of 1839.

The *Amistad* was a Spanish slave ship. While carrying a cargo of slaves from Africa to the West Indies, the slaves revolted and killed part of the crew. The ship finally drifted ashore in Connecticut. At the urging of abolitionist lawyers, state courts ruled that the Africans should be freed. Two years later the U.S. Supreme Court upheld Connecticut's verdict and the Africans were returned to their homeland.

In 1852, author Harriet Beecher Stowe, a native of Litchfield, gave abolitionism a great boost with her best-selling novel *Uncle Tom's Cabin*. Set on a Southern plantation, the book converted thousands of Americans to the antislavery cause. In the proslavery South, even possessing the book was considered dangerous.

An abolitionist with a more radical approach was Torrington-born John

First published in installments in the antislavery newspaper *National Era, Uncle Tom's Cabin* sold 300,000 copies in a few months when it appeared in book form in 1852. Stage versions of the novel were popular even after the Civil War, as this poster (above) shows.

This photograph of John Brown (right) was taken in 1850, before his abolitionist activities turned violent. Many New Englanders, however, believed the evil of slavery justified Brown's actions: When he was hung in 1859, church bells rang in antislavery towns across the state of Connecticut to honor him.

Brown. Brown became notorious in the mid-1850s for the murder of proslavery settlers in the Kansas Territory. In 1859, Brown and a handful of followers captured the federal arsenal at Harpers Ferry, Virginia, attempting to spark a slave uprising throughout the South. Quickly captured, tried, and executed, Brown was seen as a martyr by many abolitionists.

With the election of Abraham Lincoln as president in 1860, the tensions between the free North and the slave-owning South reached the breaking point. Eleven Southern states seceded from the Union to form the Confederate States of America, and the Civil War began in April 1861.

Under the firm wartime leadership of Governor William Buckingham, Connecticut contributed more than

Soldiers of a Connecticut artillery regiment pose for this 1862 photograph. As in the Revolutionary War, the state wasted no time in sending men to the fight: The first unit of Connecticut volunteers arrived in Washington, D.C., just three days after the Civil War began.

its share to the Union cause. Nearly 60,000 Connecticut men served in the Union army and navy, and about 20,000 of them were killed, wounded, or captured. The industries in the state backed up this human contribution with vast quantities of firearms, uniforms, shoes, and gunpowder.

Gideon Welles, a Glastonbury native, served as secretary of the navy in President Lincoln's cabinet. Welles, nicknamed "Father Neptune" by Lincoln, proved to be one of the Union's most effective leaders.

As the war dragged on and casualty

lists grew however, war weariness set in across the Union, and Connecticut was no exception. Opposition to the war in Connecticut was spearheaded by Thomas H. Seymour, leader of the state's "Peace Democrats"—members of the Democratic Party who wanted to negotiate peace with the Confederacy.

In 1863, Seymour ran for governor against incumbent William Buckingham. The election was seen as a test of public support for President Lincoln and his policies, and people across the Union watched as the votes were counted. Buckingham won, and Connecticut continued its strong support for the Union until the Confederacy's defeat in April 1865.

One of Gideon Welles's toughest jobs as secretary of the navy was maintaining the Union blockade of Southern ports to keep overseas aid from reaching the Confederacy. Unfortunately, the blockade wasn't very effective in the early years of the war. This cartoon pokes fun at Welles by depicting Union sailors manning washtubs while a Confederate "blockade runner" slips by.

Manufacturer to the Nation

In the half-century following the Civil War, Connecticut experienced deep and lasting change, thanks to waves of immigration from overseas. In 1865, when the state's population was nearly 500,000, three quarters of Connecticut's people were native-born Americans. By 1900, when Connecticut's population neared 1 million, 70 percent of the state's people were born overseas, or had parents of foreign birth.

The Irish, who first came to Connecticut in large numbers in the late 1840s, were joined over the years by people from many other countries. Germans and Scandinavians arrived in the decades following the Civil War. After about 1900, tens of thousands of people from Poland, Russia, Lithuania, and other eastern and central European nations came to Connecticut. The early 1900s also saw a surge of immigration from Italy to Connecticut and other northern states. Eventually, Italian Americans replaced Irish Americans as the single largest ethnic group in the state.

Connecticut truly earned the nickname "manufacturer to the nation" in the post-Civil War era. The number of manufacturers in the state jumped

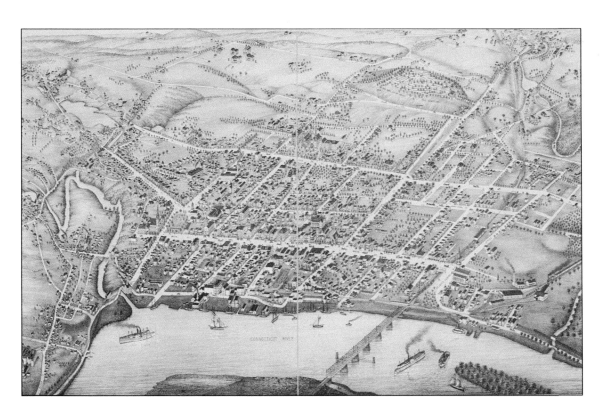

from 5,000 in 1870 to 9,000 in 1900, and the worth of the goods they produced rose from $160 million to $300 million. Even more impressive than these numbers was the sheer variety of goods produced in Connecticut.

The workers who made Connecticut's factories hum, however, often faced long hours, low pay, unsafe workplaces, and no job security. As in other industrial states, Connecticut's workers joined together into unions to win better treatment from factory owners.

In 1878, workers in New Britain organized a chapter of the Knights of Labor, which was then the largest union in the country. A decade later, labor won a major victory when the state government established a sixty-hour work week for Connecticut workers.

Along with industrialization came urbanization. The number of Connecticut people living in cities rose

Middletown on the Connecticut River became one of Connecticut's wealthiest towns in the 1700s thanks to trade with the West Indies. In 1877, when this bird's-eye view lithograph (opposite) was published, the city was booming again, this time thanks to manufacturing. Firearms, ammunition, and clothing were all turned out by Middletown's mills and factories.

This photograph (below) from the Mystic Seaport Museum shows a passenger ferry steaming up the Thames River in New London, while dockside warehouses stand ready to receive the day's catch from the city's fishing fleet. Fishing, trade, and shipbuilding brought prosperity to Connecticut's coastal towns in the late 19th century.

rapidly in the late 1800s and early 1900s. New Haven and Bridgeport were each home to more than 100,000 people by 1910, and Hartford and Waterbury passed the 50,000 mark around the same time.

Ever since colonial times, New Haven and Hartford served as "dual" capitals for Connecticut. In 1875, however, the state capital moved permanently to Hartford, and work began on a new capitol building. Completed in 1880, the new capitol is a magnificent structure of marble and granite, topped with a golden dome and set within beautiful forty-acre Bushnell Park.

During these years, the most famous resident of Hartford was Mark Twain (Samuel Langhorne Clemens's pen name), one of America's greatest writers. Twain moved to Hartford in 1870 and stayed for more than twenty years. Here Twain wrote some of his best and best-loved novels, including *The Adventures of Tom Sawyer*, *The Adventures of Huckleberry Finn*, and *A Connecticut Yankee in King Arthur's Court*.

A transplanted Westerner, Twain came to love Connecticut—although he expressed humorous frustration with the state's weather, which often changes suddenly. "In the spring I have counted one hundred and thirty-six kinds of weather inside of twenty-four hours," Twain told an audience in 1876.

The importance of agriculture in Connecticut declined as the state became an industrial powerhouse. In the early 1900s, however, Connecticut achieved success in a very specialized area of agriculture—the cultivation of wrapper tobacco, the "leaf" used to wrap cigars.

Wrapper tobacco had been grown in a small patch of the Connecticut River Valley for many years, but at the end of the 19th century, cigar makers began using wrapper tobacco imported from the East Indian island of Sumatra instead of that from Connecticut. The state's secretary of agriculture, James Wilson, decided to see if Sumatran tobacco would grow in the Connecticut Valley.

The secret, Wilson discovered, was to grow the plant under the shade of cotton cloth. When the first crop of shade-grown wrapper tobacco was harvested and cured in 1900, experts found it to be as good as the Sumatran product. Wrapper tobacco has been an important Connecticut product ever since.

When the United States entered World War I in 1917, Connecticut's manufacturers went into high gear to meet the needs of the war effort. The Winchester Company of New Haven alone turned out almost 500,000 rifles for the United States and Allied forces. Remington, Colt, and other Connecticut arms manufacturers produced about half the ammunition used by the U.S. Army in the conflict, and the state's mills and factories contributed great quantities of uniforms, gas masks, parachutes, and other military necessities.

Submarine manufacturing, soon to be an important part of the state's economy, began when the U.S. Navy chose Groton as its Atlantic Coast submarine base in 1917.

This 1890 photograph (opposite) shows a tobacco farm near Middletown. By 1900, competition from overseas forced the state's tobacco planters to adopt the new technique of shade-growing—or "farming under a blanket," as the method came to be called.

Connecticut's civilians pitched in to aid America and the Allies during World War I. In this photograph (below), women volunteers at the State Fair collect donations for a "Food for France" fund.

Good Times, Hard Times and War

Connecticut's economy went through a brief slump in the years just following World War I, as the state's industry shifted back to the production of civilian goods, and for a time unemployment was high. Connecticut was soon back on its feet, however, and the 1920s was a generally prosperous decade for the state and its people.

Part of the state's growth was fueled by a new industry: aviation. Connecticut became a major manufacturer of both aircraft and aircraft engines during the 1920s. The state's best-known engine manufacturer, Pratt & Whitney, began business with twenty-five employees in a Hartford machine

Founded by Francis Pratt and Amos Whitney as a tool-making firm in 1865, Pratt & Whitney began manufacturing aircraft engines in the mid-1920s and quickly became the industry's leader. In this 1925 photograph, workers pose with the first engine to be shipped from the company's Hartford factory.

shop in 1925. Ten years later, the company employed more than 2,000 people at its huge East Hartford plant.

The number of immigrants settling in Connecticut fell off after about 1920, when federal laws began to restrict immigration from overseas, but newcomers continued to arrive in the state.

African Americans from the rural South came in the early 1900s to work on the tobacco farms of the Connecticut River Valley, and their numbers increased during the wartime industrial boom of 1917–18. French-speaking Canadians, too, began to form an important ethnic group in the state. By 1930, more than 100,000 French Canadians lived in Connecticut. Many found work in the textile mills of the northeastern part of the state.

Despite the great social change that took place in Connecticut during the late 19th and early 20th centuries, the state's politics lagged behind. Most of the people who lived in Connecticut's cities and worked in its factories tended to belong to the Democratic Party. Nevertheless, the Republican Party, which drew much of its support from rural, native-born Yankees and prosperous industrialists, dominated the state government from the Civil War until 1930.

This situation occurred, in part, because the 1818 state constitution based representation in the state legislature on towns, rather than on overall population. Each Connecticut town had at least one representative in the state legislature, but no community, no matter how big, had more than two. Thus, a rural village of a couple of hundred people had the same representation in the legislature as a big city like Hartford or Bridgeport. Most of Connecticut's small towns were Republican strongholds, so it was easy for the party to control the state government.

Another reason for "Yankee Republican" domination was the party's efficient statewide organization. From

This Polish couple—laborers on a Connecticut Valley tobacco farm—were among the thousands of immigrants from Eastern and Central Europe who came to the state in the first decades of the 20th century.

1910 until his death in 1937, the state party was controlled by chairman J. Henry Roraback, one of the legendary political "bosses" of the 20th century. Roraback ran the party, and thus the state government, with an iron hand. He decided personally who would receive nominations for office and which laws would be introduced in the legislature.

It took a grave crisis—the Great Depression—to end one-party rule in Connecticut. Touched off by the 1929 collapse of the New York Stock Exchange, the Depression spread unemployment and economic hardship across the nation as banks failed and factories shut their doors. The Depression was especially damaging in northeastern industrial states like Connecticut.

In 1930, as the effects of the economic slump began to reach Connecticut, a Yale professor named Wilbur H. Cross decided to challenge Roraback and the Republicans. Winning the Democratic nomination for the governor's race, Cross defeated the Republican candidate and took office in 1931 just as the worst years of the Depression began. By 1932, one in four Connecticut workers was unemployed. In some areas of the state the jobless rate ran higher than 50 percent.

Working together with the legislature, where the Republicans still formed the majority, "Uncle Toby" Cross worked hard to save Connect-icut's people from the misery caused by the Depression. During his eight years in office, Cross succeeded in passing state laws providing aid to the unemployed and the elderly, as well as ending child labor and establishing a minimum wage.

As if the Depression wasn't bad enough, nature hit Connecticut with two major blows during the 1930s. In 1936, the Connecticut River flooded, washing out the east side of Hartford and causing more than $25 million in property damage. Two years later, a tropical hurricane slammed through New England. The storm claimed eighty-five lives in Connecticut and cut a path of destruction across the state's coastline.

The coming of World War II in December 1941 revived Connecticut's depression-ravaged economy. As they had done in every major conflict since the Revolutionary War, Connecticut's people and businesses came together to perform miracles of productivity for the war effort.

The state's factories filled $8 billion in government orders for military hardware—everything from aircraft and submarines to ball bearings and ammunition. Connecticut was the single most productive state during the war years on the basis of goods produced per person.

More than 210,000 men and women from Connecticut served in the armed forces during the conflict, and nearly 6,000 gave their lives.

A shipyard worker (right) at the Electric Boat Company in Groton takes a look at the hull of a submarine under construction—one of the seventy-five submarines produced in Connecticut during the war years.

Of the many Connecticut residents who served in World War II, one would become president of the United States. George Bush, shown here (below) in his navy torpedo-bomber in 1944, won a Distinguished Flying Cross for completing a mission after his aircraft was hit by enemy fire. Bush attended Yale University after the war.

The Rise of the Suburbs

Connecticut's growth in the decades following World War II was phenomenal. Between 1945 and 1970, the state's population increased 75 percent—from about 1.7 million to 3 million.

Many of Connecticut's new residents made homes in Fairfield County in the southwest corner of the state. The county's closeness to New York City made it a favorite suburb for thousands of businesspeople who commuted to jobs in Manhattan each day. Having a Connecticut address also held another attraction—unlike New York, Connecticut had no state personal income tax.

Suburbanization was an important trend in the rest of the state, too. The children of immigrants who had worked in the mills and factories of urban Connecticut could now afford to move their families to the suburbs that sprang up around Hartford, New Haven, and other cities.

As these people moved away from Connecticut's cities, new arrivals took their place. African-American migration to Connecticut increased after World War II; by the 1960s, African Americans made up about 7 percent of the state's population. More than 125,000 Hispanics, many of them from Puerto Rico, arrived after about 1960.

When Connecticut's middle class moved to the suburbs, they took their tax dollars with them. Many businesses, too, found it profitable to move away from crowded city centers. By the mid-1950s, Connecticut's major cities were suffering from financial problems and slowing economic growth.

To fight this trend, politicians joined with businesses and labor unions in ambitious programs of urban renewal. This meant clearing away old, decayed areas and financing the construction of new buildings and facilities to attract jobs, shoppers, and residents.

In New Haven, Mayor Richard Lee (who served from 1954 to 1970) oversaw the development of the Chapel Square Mall, a downtown shopping area linked to major roadways. In 1960, Hartford businesses put up most of the $40 million needed to build Constitution Plaza, an office-hotel complex that transformed the city's run-down riverfront. Some critics, however, argued that in the long run the costs of these projects outweighed the benefits they brought to the community.

Economically, the years between the end of World War II and the mid-1960s were prosperous ones for many of Connecticut's businesses. The cold war was on, government

spending on military hardware was high, and the state's defense-related industries boomed. In Groton, the Electric Boat division of the General Dynamics corporation built nuclear-powered submarines for the U.S. Navy, starting with the USS *Nautilus* in 1954. Pratt & Whitney turned out jet engines for military aircraft, and the Sikorsky Company (later United Technologies) in Stratford became one of the nation's leading helicopter manufacturers.

Two Connecticut residents were honored for cultural achievements during the postwar years. In 1947, Danbury-born composer Charles Ives won the Pulitzer Prize in music for his *Third Symphony.* Many of Ives's unique compositions have New England themes.

Designed to revitalize New Haven's downtown, the Chapel Square Mall replaced a depressed commercial district with new shops, businesses, and a pedestrian plaza.

Poet Wallace Stevens won both the National Book Award and the Pulitzer Prize for his *Collected Poems* in 1954. Stevens was also vice president of a major Hartford insurance agency for twenty years. Many of his fellow executives didn't know about his literary career until he received the Pulitzer Prize.

Connecticut politics experienced two great changes in the late 1950s and 1960s. In 1959, the state did away with county governments. The new system placed all government functions with the state or with local (township) governments.

Six years later, a new state constitution was adopted to replace the constitution of 1818. Because of a U.S. Supreme Court decision, the 1965 constitution reorganized representation in the state legislature on the basis of "one person, one vote." This finally ended the old system of representation by towns.

The son of a Civil War bandleader, Charles Ives (above, left) is considered by many critics to be one of America's greatest composers. Ives's unique compositions—including the orchestral work *Three Places in New England* and the *Concord Piano Sonata*, inspired by the writings of New England authors—received little attention until late in his life.

This photograph (left) shows the Connecticut state capitol, designed by Richard Upjohn. The building became the seat of government in 1879. The previous state house was the first in the country and was the center of Connecticut government from 1636 to 1878.

A State of Contrasts

Connecticut showed two very different sides of itself during the 1960s and 1970s. On the one hand, Connecticut seemed to be a model state. By the 1970s Connecticut was the second-wealthiest state on the basis of average income per person, and it rose to first place in the next decade. The state continued to attract new residents, although population growth slowed significantly after 1970. Many of its industries, especially those connected to the military, continued to prosper.

On the other hand, unemployment rose in some areas as manufacturing became less important to the country's overall economy. For example, many of Connecticut's traditional businesses—like the brass industry in Waterbury—involved metal. As plastics replaced metal in many products, foundries and mills laid off workers and shut down.

Many of the social problems that cropped up after World War II also grew worse during this time. Although they were successful in some ways, the urban renewal programs begun in the 1950s didn't stop the decline of Connecticut's cities. Bridgeport, Hartford, and New Haven all experienced economic slowdowns, tension between people of different races, and general decay. So did many of the old industrial towns in the Connecticut River Valley and elsewhere in the state. More and more, Connecticut became a state of suburbs that were generally middle-class or wealthy and white, and cities that were increasingly poor or working-class and mostly African American and Hispanic.

Connecticut has always been considered a quiet, conservative state, but it still experienced the unrest that swept through the nation in the late 1960s. In the summer of 1967, race riots broke out in Hartford's North End, and similar disturbances took place in Bridgeport, New Britain, and other communities.

In New Haven, home of Yale University, the Vietnam War caused tension between the university and townspeople. Many of the city's residents resented the antiwar attitude held by many of the school's students and professors. The situation grew worse when Yale president Kingman Brewster claimed that Bobby Seale, an African-American political radical charged with murder, could not get a fair trial in the city. Many New Havenites took this as an insult. (In fact, Seale was acquitted of the charge in 1971 by a mostly white New Haven jury.)

Calmness and a willingness to compromise, however, have always been a part of Connecticut life. These qualities helped Connecticut find ways to improve conditions for the state's people, even though many tough problems—like the decline of the cities—had no easy solutions.

In the 1960s and 1970s, for example, Connecticut's state government passed pioneering environmental protection laws and ended minimum charges for utilities like electricity and water for the state's poorest citizens. Concern over the dangers of nuclear power and radioactive waste led the state to ban construction of nuclear power plants in 1979.

In the capitol, the 1970s was the decade of Ella Grasso. The daughter of a baker who came to Connecticut from Italy, Grasso served as Connecticut's secretary of state before becoming governor in 1974. She was the first woman governor elected in her own right—all previous woman governors had followed their husbands into office, or had been appointed.

Grasso was a Democrat, but she earned the support of many Republicans with her conservative financial views. During her five years in office, Grasso firmly opposed calls for the state government to adopt a personal income tax.

Even if some disagreed with her policies, Connecticut's voters respected Grasso's honesty and practical approach to government. Cancer forced her to resign from office in 1980; when she died the following year, the entire state mourned.

Despite the ambitious urban renewal programs of the 1950s and 1960s, and the ongoing efforts of community groups and local businesses, Connecticut's capital city now struggles with problems of crime and unemployment. In 1994, Hartford (opposite) was ranked among the ten poorest major cities in the United States.

This beautifully restored colonial house (above) is typical of the homes to be found in Connecticut's wealthier communities. In Greenwich—a suburb especially popular with commuters to New York City—the average house price rose to more than $500,000 in the early 1990s.

Ella Grasso (right), born in Windsor Locks as Ella Rosa Giovanna Oliva Tambussi, was the first woman in America to be elected governor in her own right. Grasso served in the State Assembly and was secretary of state before becoming governor in 1974.

Connecticut Today

Connecticut welcomed the 1980s with yet another groundbreaking political event—the election of Thirman Milner as mayor of Hartford. Milner was the first African American to become mayor of a major New England city. His election reflected the growing political influence of African Americans in Connecticut.

Fairfield County enjoyed a boom in the early 1980s as twenty-five major corporations, with a total worth of $100 billion, moved their headquarters to the area. The county's new status even led to "suburbanization in reverse"—instead of living in Connecticut and commuting to New York, thousands of people who lived in New York and New Jersey now commuted to jobs in Stamford or Darien.

Connecticut's economy in general was fairly strong during the 1980s, especially after the national economy picked up in the middle of the decade. Defense spending remained a vital part of the state's economic picture— among the states, only California's defense plants produced more hardware for the U.S. military. With its well-educated work force and closeness to research centers in New York and the rest of New England, Connecticut also attracted many "high tech" computer and telecommunications companies.

As the 1980s gave way to the 1990s, however, Connecticut entered its worst economic crisis since the Depression of the 1930s. Part of the problem was old news—manufacturing, the major source of the state's wealth since the 19th century, continued to decline. The nationwide recession that began around 1990 made this long-standing problem even worse in Connecticut.

The end of the cold war was another factor. As the tensions between the Soviet Union and the United States fell, so did defense spending. For Connecticut, this meant layoffs at defense-related companies across the state. The worst hit was Electric Boat

in Groton, which faced a drastic cutback in production of nuclear submarines. By the end of 1991 Electric Boat had laid off 1,500 of its 13,000 employees.

The statewide crisis made conditions in the cities even more desperate —and few cities in the nation were as desperate as Bridgeport in the early 1990s. In 1991, the city actually declared bankruptcy—the largest American city ever to do so. Once a thriving industrial town, Connecticut's largest city was now filled with closed-down factories and burned-out businesses, and gunfire from drug dealers' battles echoed down deserted streets. The city's murder rate in 1993 was four times the national average. Unfortunately, the state government had little money to spare for its trou-

By 1980, African Americans and Hispanics made up more than half the population of Hartford. The following year, Thirman L. Milner (opposite) was elected as Hartford's mayor— the first African American to serve as mayor of a large New England city. Later in the decade, former state senator John C. Daniels became New Haven's first black mayor.

The Maritime Center at Norwalk, built in 1988 in a restored 19th-century waterfront factory, is a classic example of the economic revitalization of Connecticut cities. In this photograph (above), a young boy watches a shark aquarium in awe.

bled cities. By 1990, the gap between the state's income and expenses approached the breaking point.

In that year, Lowell P. Weicker, Jr., won election as governor. A Republican who had rarely paid attention to party lines as a U.S. representative and senator, Weicker ran as an independent candidate. Upon taking office in 1991, he proved his independence by doing something a string of Connecticut governors had refused to do—he introduced a state personal income tax of 4.5 percent. The legislature defeated the measure four times before it finally won passage.

Weicker's move angered many state residents; an antitax rally at the capitol drew 40,000 people. Critics charged that the tax would just add to Connecticut's cost of living, already one of the highest in the country, and do nothing to revive the state's economy. Weicker and his supporters argued that the state desperately needed a more predictable source of money to plug a $1 billion budget deficit, and the governor promised to combine the tax with deep spending cuts.

The state government also began an innovative partnership with the Mashantucket Pequots, the surviving descendants of the once-mighty Native American nation. After a federal court ruled that the Pequots could operate a casino on tribal land, the state government agreed to let the Pequots operate slot machines. As part of a plan to contain legalized gambling in Connecticut, the legislature agreed that it would collect a portion of the Foxwoods Casino's profits (25 percent) only as long as it did not authorize any other casinos to open shop.

In 1993, the deal brought the state $113 million. Most of that money went to Connecticut's cities and towns. The Foxwoods Casino, just outside Mystic, provided jobs for more than 8,000 people.

In late 1993 the state began to pull out of the recession. More than 11,000 new jobs were created during the first half of 1994, and many new businesses began to spring up. Thanks to strong support from the State Department of Economic Development, programs were also initiated to help businesses diversify by decreasing their reliance on the defense, insurance, and banking industries.

The problems of the recession made it easy to forget Connecticut's great strengths. For one thing, much of the beauty of the land remains, making it one of the most popular tourist destinations. Many people from New York City take refuge in Connecticut on the weekends and buy second homes there. More than 100 state parks preserve some of the wilderness that greeted the first settlers more than 350 years ago.

An even greater resource is the inventive spirit of the Connecticut people. Connecticut's rich history certainly proves that "Yankee ingenuity" continues to thrive in the state. That legendary ingenuity will do much to help the state solve the problems of the 1990s, and to meet the challenges the future holds.

Lowell Weicker (right) began his political career with his election to the Connecticut legislature in 1962; five years later he was elected to the U.S. House of Representatives, and he moved to the Senate in 1970. Weicker's willingness to go against his own party and to take controversial positions—such as his support for a state income tax when he was governor—have made him one of the nation's best-known politicians.

A family enjoys a hay ride after picking pumpkins at one of Connecticut's harvest festivals in this photograph (below). Autumn is one of the state's busiest seasons, as people come to admire Connecticut's beautiful fall foliage.

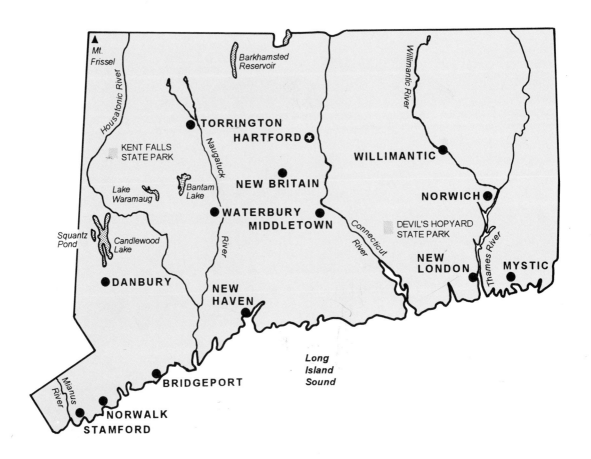

Land area:
> 5,018 square miles, of which 146 are inland water. Ranks 48th in size.

Major rivers:
> The Connecticut; the Housatonic; the Mianus; the Naugatuck; the Thames; the Willimantic.

> **Highest point:** Mt. Frissel, 2,380 ft.

Climate:
> Average January temperature: 27°F
> Average July temperature: 74°F

Major bodies of water:
> Bantam Lake; Barkhamsted Reservoir; Candlewood Lake (artificial); Squantz Pond; Lake Waramaug.

Population: 3,280,959 (1992)
Rank: 27th
   1900: 908,420
   1790: 237,946

Population of major cities (1990):
Bridgeport:	141,686
Hartford:	139,739
New Haven:	130,474
Waterbury:	108,961
Stamford:	108,056
Norwalk:	78,331
New Britain:	75,491

Ethnic breakdown by percentage (1990):
White	83.8%
African American	7.9%
Hispanic	6.5%
Asian/Pacific Islander	1.5%
Native American	0.2%
Other	0.1%

Economy:
   Financing, insurance, real estate, manufacturing (weapons, jet engines, helicopters, submarines, and electrical equipment), agriculture (eggs and poultry, dairy products, and apples), horticulture (greenhouse and plant nurseries), and tourism.

State government:
   Legislature: The General Assembly consists of a 151-member House of Representatives and a 36-member Senate, all of whom are elected for 2-year terms.
   Governor: The governor is elected for a 4-year term.
   Courts: Superior court, appellate court, and supreme court. Major criminal and civil cases are tried by the 131-member superior court.
State capital: Hartford

State Flag

Adopted in 1897, Connecticut's flag features the state seal enclosed in a shield against a blue background. The state motto appears in a scroll beneath the shield.

State Seal

Connecticut's seal shows three grapevines. Around the border are the Latin words *Sigilum Republicæ Connecticutensis*—"The Seal of the Connecticut Republic."

State Motto

Connecticut's motto refers to its colonial heritage: *Qui Transtulit Sustanit*, Latin for "He who transplanted still sustains."

State Nickname

The "Constitution State"; also known as the "Nutmeg State" and the "Land of Steady Habits."

Places

American Clock and Watch Museum, Bristol

American Indian Archaeological Institute, Washington

Bush-Holley House, Cos Cob

Charles Ives Center, Danbury

Connecticut Arboretum, New London

Connecticut Historical Society, Hartford

Devil's Hopyard State Park, East Haddam

Dinosaur State Park, Rocky Hill

Eugene O'Neill Memorial Theater Center, Waterford

Fort Griswold Monument, Groton

Gillette Castle, Hadlyme

Harriet Beecher Stowe House, Hartford

Henry Whitfield House, Guilford

Jonathan Trumbull House, Lebanon

Keeler Tavern, Ridgefield

Kent Falls State Park, North Kent

Kent Furnace, Kent

Lighthouse Point Park, New Haven

Lock 12 Historical Park, Cheshire

Lock Museum of America, Terryville

Mark Twain House, Hartford

Massacoh Plantation, Simsbury

to See

Mattatuck Museum,
Waterbury

Museum of
Connecticut
History, Hartford

Mystic Seaport and
Aquarium, Mystic

Nathan Hale Home,
Coventry

Noah Webster
House and Museum,
West Hartford

Norwalk Maritime
Center, Norwalk

Old Newgate
Prison, East Granby

Old State House,
Hartford

P. T. Barnum
Museum, Bridgeport

Prudence Crandall
House, Canterbury

Putnam Memorial
State Park, Bethel

Sawmill Park,
Ledyard

Tapping Reeve
House, Litchfield

The Bruce Museum,
Greenwich

Union Station,
Canaan

United States Coast
Guard Academy,
New London

USS *Nautilus*
Memorial, Groton

Wadsworth
Atheneum, Hartford

Whitney Museum
of American Art,
Stamford

Yale Center for
British Art,
New Haven

Yale University Art
Gallery, New Haven

Peabody Museum,
New Haven

Yale University,
New Haven

State Flower

The white- or rose-colored flower of the mountain laurel, an evergreen shrub, is Connecticut's state flower. This beautiful but poisonous plant can reach a height of about thirty feet.

State Bird

Early colonists named the American robin after the European robin of their homeland. The American robin has a gray back and russet-brown breast.

State Tree

Connecticut's state tree is the white oak. This magnificent hardwood tree is about 100 feet tall when fully grown.

Connecticut History

1614 Adrian Block explores Connecticut for the Netherlands

1633 First Dutch and English settlements established

1636 Hartford, Wethersfield, and Windsor form Connecticut Colony

1637 Pequot War

1638 New Haven Colony established

1639 Fundamental Orders of Connecticut adopted

1665 New Haven incorporated into Connecticut Colony

1687 Sir Edmund Andros fails to unite New York and Connecticut

1701 Yale University founded

1764 *The Hartford Courant* begins publication

1765 Sons of Liberty founded in Connecticut to resist British rule

1781 Benedict Arnold leads British assaults on Groton and New London

1784 Connecticut begins abolition of slavery

1788 Connecticut becomes the fifth state to ratify the Constitution

1833 Prudence Crandall opens short-lived school for African-American girls

1836 Samuel Colt patents his revolver

1839 Vulcanizing process for rubber developed by Charles Goodyear

American

1492 Christopher Columbus reaches the New World

1607 Jamestown (Virginia) founded by English colonists

1620 *Mayflower* arrives at Plymouth (Massachusetts)

1754–63 French and Indian War

1765 Parliament passes Stamp Act

1775–83 Revolutionary War

1776 Signing of the Declaration of Independence

1788–90 First congressional elections

1791 Bill of Rights added to U.S. Constitution

1803 Louisiana Purchase

1812–14 War of 1812

1820 Missouri Compromise

1836 Battle of the Alamo, Texas

1846–48 Mexican-American War

1849 California Gold Rush

1860 South Carolina secedes from Union

1861–65 Civil War

1862 Lincoln signs Homestead Act

1863 Emancipation Proclamation

1865 President Lincoln assassinated (April 14)

1865–77 Reconstruction in the South

1866 Civil Rights bill passed

1881 President James Garfield shot (July 2)

History

1896 First Ford automobile is made

1898–99 Spanish-American War

1901 President William McKinley is shot (Sept. 6)

1917 U.S. enters World War I

1922 Nineteenth Amendment passed, giving women the vote

1929 U.S. stock market crash; Great Depression begins

1933 Franklin D. Roosevelt becomes president; begins New Deal

1941 Japanese attack Pearl Harbor (Dec. 7); U.S. enters World War II

1945 U.S. drops atomic bomb on Hiroshima and Nagasaki; Japan surrenders, ending World War II

1963 President Kennedy assassinated (November 22)

1964 Civil Rights Act passed

1965–73 Vietnam War

1968 Martin Luther King, Jr., shot in Memphis (April 4)

1974 President Richard Nixon resigns because of Watergate scandal

1979–81 Hostage crisis in Iran: 52 Americans held captive for 444 days

1989 End of U.S.-Soviet cold war

1991 Gulf War

1993 U.S. signs North American Free Trade Agreement with Canada and Mexico

Connecticut History

1842 Wadsworth Atheneum opens in Hartford; first free art museum in U.S.

1878 World's first commercial telephone network begins operating in New Haven

1917 U.S. Naval Base opens at Groton

1938 East Coast hurricane claims 85 lives

1943 Connecticut becomes first state to form a civil rights commission

1944 Fire at Ringling Bros. Circus outside Hartford kills 167 people

1954 Launching of first nuclear-powered submarine at Groton

1955 More than 100 people killed in flooding of Connecticut River

1960 Connecticut abolishes county governments throughout state

1965 New state constitution adopted

1967–68 Riots in Hartford, Bridgeport, and other cities

1974 Ella Grasso elected governor; first woman governor elected in her own right in U.S.

1981 Thirman Milner becomes mayor of Hartford; first black mayor of a New England city

1991 Connecticut government imposes state income tax

1994 Connecticut receives record snowfall, exceeding 85 inches

Thomas Hooker (1586–1647) A Puritan leader, Hooker and his congregation migrated from the Massachusetts Bay Colony to Connecticut and settled at present-day Hartford.

Uncas (c. 1606–c. 1683) Leader of the Mohegans, Uncas joined with Connecticut's English colonists to crush the Pequots in 1637. Uncas also sided with the colonists in King Philip's War (1675–76).

Roger Sherman (1721–93) A signer of both the Declaration of Independence and the Constitution, Sherman helped write the "Connecticut Compromise" that became part of the U.S. Constitution.

Ethan Allen (1738–89) This Litchfield-born soldier and pioneer helped capture Fort Ticonderoga from the British in May 1775. Allen spent much of his life working to make Vermont an independent state.

Oliver Ellsworth (1745–1807) Ellsworth cosponsored the "Connecticut Compromise" at the Constitutional Convention. The Windsor native also served as chief justice of the United States (1796–1800).

Nathan Hale (1755–76) A Yale-educated schoolteacher, Hale was captured by the British in New York City while on a spying mission and hanged.

Noah Webster (1758–1843) West Hartford-born Webster helped standardize American English with his *American Dictionary of the English Language* (1828).

Eli Whitney (1765–1825) One of the most influential American inventors, Whitney invented the cotton gin in 1793, shortly after graduating from Yale. Whitney also developed mass-production methods that had a great impact on American manufacturing.

Thomas Gallaudet (1783–1851) After studying methods of teaching the deaf in Britain and France, Gallaudet founded the American Asylum for Deaf-Mutes in Hartford in 1817.

Emma Hart Willard (1787–1870) A major innovator in the field of education for women, Willard founded schools in New York and Connecticut, wrote many textbooks, and helped train the first generation of professional women teachers.

John Brown (1800–59) A native of Torrington, Brown was a radical abolitionist. He was executed after seizing the federal arsenal at Harpers Ferry, Virginia, in an attempt to inspire a slave uprising throughout the South.

Samuel Colt

Charles Goodyear (1800–60) In 1839, Goodyear developed the process of vulcanization, which made rubber a practical substance for use in everyday articles.

Prudence Crandall (1803–90) Crandall founded

a school for African-American girls at Canterbury in 1833, but an angry mob shut the school down. In 1994, the state legislature nominated her to be Connecticut's first State Heroine.

P. T. (Phineas Taylor) Barnum (1810–91) This legendary showman and promoter was born in Bethel and lived in Bridgeport for much of his life. Barnum also served one term as Bridgeport's mayor and several terms as a member of the state legislature.

Samuel Colt (1814–62) Colt invented one of the first practical repeating firearms, the Colt revolver, in 1836.

Mark Twain (1835–1910) One of America's greatest and best-loved authors, Twain wrote many of his most enduring works (including *A Connecticut Yankee in King Arthur's Court*) while living in Hartford. Mark Twain was the pen name of Samuel Langhorne Clemens.

Charles Ives (1874–1954) Now considered one of America's greatest composers, Ives's work was little known until late in his life. Much of the Danbury native's music was inspired by New England themes.

Wallace Stevens (1879–1955) While working as an insurance executive in Hartford, Stevens published many books of poetry. His *Collected Poems* (1954) won both the Pulitzer Prize and the American Book Award.

Eugene O'Neill (1888–1953) This Nobel Prize-winning playwright spent much of his early life in New London; the city is the setting for *A Moon for the Misbegotten* (1947), one of his best-known plays.

Igor Sikorsky (1889–1972) A Russian-born engineer, Sikorsky developed many new aircraft designs, including some of the first practical helicopters, at his Stratford factory.

Clare Booth Luce (1903–87) After successful careers as a magazine editor and playwright, Luce represented Connecticut in the House of Representatives (1943–47) and served as U.S. ambassador to Italy (1953–57).

Ella Grasso (1919–81) Born in Windsor Locks, Ella Tambussi Grasso, a Democrat, served in a number of state

Clare Booth Luce

offices and as a U.S. representative before winning election as governor in 1974.

Katharine Hepburn (b. 1909) Winner of three Academy Awards, this distinguished film and stage actress is a native of Hartford.

Abraham Ribicoff (b. 1910) This New Britain-born politician's long public career included stints in Congress, as governor, and as secretary of health, education, and welfare.

Ralph Nader (b. 1934) Born in Winsted, Nader became America's most famous consumer advocate with the 1965 publication of *Unsafe at Any Speed*, a critical look at the automobile industry.

Pictures in this volume:

Bridgeport Public Library: 31

Connecticut Historical Society: 38

Connecticut Department of Tourism: 2, 46 (bottom), 49 (top), 51, 53 (bottom)

Connecticut State Library/The Ruebens Studio: 49 (bottom)

Dover: 9 (top), 14, 17 (bottom), 25, 28 (top)

Governor's Office: 53 (top)

Hartford Convention Center: 48

Library of Congress: 9 (bottom), 10, 11, 12, 17 (top), 19, 21 (top), 22, 24, 27, 28 (bottom), 29, 33 (both), 35, 36, 46 (top), 60, 61

Litchfield Historical Society: 7

Media Projects, Inc.: 15, 21 (bottom), 23

Jim Michaud, *The Journal Inquirer*: 50

Mystic Seaport Museum: 37

National Archives: 34, 39, 41, 43 (top)

Pratt & Whitney: 40

Rouse New Haven Shopping Center, Inc.: 45

White House: 43 (bottom)

About the author:

Charles A. Wills is a writer, editor, and consultant specializing in American history. He has written, edited, or contributed to more than thirty books, including many volumes in The Millbrook Press's *American Albums from the Collections of the Library of Congress* and *State Historical Albums* series. Wills lives in Dutchess County, New York.

Suggested reading:

Carpenter, Allan. *The New Enchantment of America: Connecticut*. Chicago: Childrens Press, 1979.

Fradin, Dennis. *The Connecticut Colony*. Chicago: Childrens Press, 1990.

Gelman, Amy. *Hello USA: Connecticut*. Minneapolis: Lerner Publications, 1991.

Kent, Deborah. *America the Beautiful: Connecticut*. Chicago: Childrens Press, 1990.

Ritchie, David. *Connecticut: Off the Beaten Path*. Old Saybrook, CT: Globe Pequot, 1994.

For more information contact:

The Connecticut Historical Society
1 Elizabeth Street
Hartford, CT 06105
(203) 236-5621

Connecticut Department of Economic Development/Tourism Division
865 Brook Street
Rocky Hill, CT 06067
(800) 282-6863

INDEX